COME TO THE RIVER

MARK RUSSELL has published three full collections prior to *Come to the River*: *Men Who Repeat Themselves* (erbacce press, 2022), *Shopping for Punks* (Hesterglock, 2017), and *Spearmint & Rescue* (Pindrop, 2016). His pamphlets are published by Red Ceilings, tall-lighthouse, and Kattywompus. He won the Magma Poetry Judge's Prize in 2020, and the erbacce-poetry prize in 2022. His poems have been published in a variety of magazines and journals, including Stand, Shearsman, Poetry Wales, The Manchester Review, The Rialto, Tears in the Fence, The Interpreter's House, Molly Bloom, Gutter, New Writing Scotland, Poetry Salzburg Review, Tentacular, and Blackbox Manifold.

Come to the River

MARK RUSSELL

Downingfield Press

Text copyright © 2024 Mark Russell. Typesetting and book design
copyright © 2024 Downingfield Press Proprietary Limited.
All rights reserved.

Without limiting the rights under copyright reserved above, in
accordance with the Copyright Act 1968 (Commonwealth of
Australia) no part of this publication may be reproduced, stored in or
introduced into a retrieval system, or transmitted, in any form or by
any means (electronic, mechanical, xerographic, recording, or
otherwise), without the prior written permission of the copyright
owner and the publisher of this book, except for brief passages
quoted for the purpose of criticism or review.

Mark Russell asserts their right to be
known as the author of this work.

Book design by M. G. Mader.

ISBN 978-1-7635569-3-5 (paperback)

First published February 2023.
Acquired and published October 2024 by

Downingfield Press Proprietary Limited
Suite 346 / 585 Little Collins Street
Melbourne Victoria 3000
Australia

For a full list of addresses and contact information, visit
global.downingfield.com

Downingfield Press undertakes its work on the traditional lands of
the Wurundjeri people of the Kulin Nation and pays respect to Elders
past, present, and emerging.

A catalogue record for this
work is available from the
National Library of Australia

for Karen and David

ACKNOWLEDGEMENTS

My thanks are due to the editors of the following publications where some of these poems, or versions of them, first appeared: *Abridged, Anthropocene, The Café Irreal, The Fortnightly Review, Molly Bloom, The Tangerine,* and *Tears in the Fence.*

PROLOGUE: KATHRINE SUBMITS

I was wandering around my classroom thinking about the fresh pasta with basil and walnut pesto I'd eaten the previous evening, when I passed Kathrine's desk. She had been hard at work for much of the morning, and she handed me her completed task. 'What is this?' I said, taking it from her. 'It's a plate of croutons fried lightly in olive oil and garlic, each of which has a word inscribed upon it.' I fell in love with Kathrine's latest novel straight away, but felt the necessity not to show it. 'I shall need a magnifying glass,' I said, rather huffily, having put away my childish implements many years ago. 'I have brought one with me,' she said, reaching into her bag and bringing out my favourite magnifying glass. 'Where did you find it?' I said, beginning to weep. 'It was just lying about in this dream, so I picked it up. I didn't realise it was yours until this very moment.'

DAISY IN THE LIGHT

'Good afternoon, Mr Fredericks,' the young woman on the desk said. I don't know how she knew my name. I was sure we'd never met. Her name tag said 'Daisy'. 'That will be thirty-four dollars,' she said, tapping something into her phone. 'I only have pounds sterling, Daisy.' 'How did you know my name?' she said, 'I'm sure we've never met.' Before I could answer, she popped a boiled sweet into her mouth. 'People often say I look like a Daisy,' she said a little incoherently. 'Will you take a card?' I said. She smiled and took my card. 'Is my nose bright orange today?' she said. I took a good long look at her face. It certainly had a tinge to it. 'More of a yellow, I'd say.' She smiled. White rays began to appear around her face, emanating from the central flowerhead of her nose. I could feel my brow begin to sweat. She swirled the boiled sweet around. It clicked against her teeth. I thought I was going to faint. 'It's a trick of the light,' she said. I breathed heavily with relief. Daisy handed me a tissue. 'You should stop looking at me now,' she said.

WINTER MOON

It had been a long time since I'd had a smoke, so long in fact, I doubted I'd ever smoked. The good thing about smokers is that they welcome other smokers, ex-smokers, and non-smokers into their fold. Their generosity toward one another is legendary. Eight of us were standing outside, just to the left of the revolving doors. 'Bernie' offered me a pink cigarette. 'I used to enjoy sitting on the leather banquettes at Bemelmans sipping a Black Russian and smoking a cocktail Sobranie,' he said. Three delegates from Romania were discussing the shape and brightness of the night's moon. From my fractured understanding of the Balkan languages, they seemed to think that despite its fullness and palpable fertility, they were tired after their long journey and were going to retire early. When I relayed this translation to Bernie, he was downcast. 'What's up, Bernie?' I said. 'My name's not Bernie,' he said, pulling off his name tag and throwing it into a shabby-looking shrub. 'I found that in a bowl of custard. I don't like my own name.' I hadn't the heart to ask him what his real name was, nor why he disliked it. As we finished our cigarettes, I started to develop a creeping antagonism toward my own name. Bernie sensed it. 'It only hurts when the sun goes down,' he said. His honesty was uplifting. We stared across the water to the lights of the BBC headquarters and the prospect of our own long winters. 'It's like an eternal flame, isn't it?' he said.

EXCHANGING GLANCES

I must have dropped off after brushing my teeth because my mouth and chin were covered in a dry white film. The bed hadn't yet been made, so I figured the rustling sound in the bathroom was the chambermaid. I didn't want to disturb her, so I poured a little water from a plastic bottle of Evian into my hand and wiped my face clean. 'In here, Mark,' a man's voice called. 'Now you're awake, can you bring me a towel?' he said. There were three towels of differing sizes on the chair. He sounded like a big man, so I picked up the largest, pushed the door open ajar staying well to the side so that I couldn't see him or what he was doing, and held the towel out as far as I could. 'What's wrong? You've seen it all before,' he laughed, taking the towel from me. I looked around the room and could see none of my own clothes or possessions, nor my travelling bag. There was, however, a pile of name tags on the desk. I flicked through them quickly: Elias, Changying, Wendy, Sasha, du Plessis, Concordia, Bob Jennings, Graeme, von Himmel, Kingsley, Adedayo, Carter the Unstoppable Sex Machine, Steve from Accounts, Jenny…There were dozens. I stuffed them into my pockets and left the room as quickly as possible, though I had somehow picked up a slight hamstring strain which impeded my progress. It felt good to be in the corridor. It felt like a new start.

BY THE DAWN'S EARLY LIGHT

There was a knock on the door. I looked at my watch. 4.17am. 'Hotel security!' a voice cried from outside. 'Open up!' Fortunately, I had emptied the minibar of all food and drink, so instead of undressing and sleeping in the buff, which is my preferred state, I was groggy, indolent, and fully clothed. It is better to look dishevelled than to be stark bollock-naked in public. That's the essential difference between consciousness and dreamtime. I was still thanking my lucky stars when hotel security broke down the door and rushed into my room. 'Who are you?' the short, blonde-haired man said. 'I'm Cheque Book Larry,' I said. 'No, you're not,' he said. 'You're right,' I said, 'I'm Avocado Dave.' 'Listen, buddy,' the tall dark-haired woman said, 'we happen to know who you are. We found your card on Daisy's body.' I tried to explain that I'd given her my card to pay for something at Reception. 'What did you buy?' she said. 'I don't know, parking maybe?' 'Thirty-four bucks for parking? Don't bust my balls, Bernie. You can't buy a prayer for less than a hundred and fifty-three bucks in this place.' A voice from the hallway said, 'Hotel security. Is everything all right in there?' We all stiffened, menacingly. 'Which one of you killed Daisy?' I hissed. 'Daisy? Daisy's not dead,' the short man said. I realised my mistake at once. It was the classic mistake. Believe nothing until you see the body.

AWKWARD, WITH PORRIDGE

I had never eaten such a delicious breakfast in my life. It was a rich, creamy porridge sweetened lightly with honey and suffused with red and purple berries. I went up to the bar to refill my coffee when I saw Daisy reading the morning papers at a corner table. 'Daisy!' I said. 'Are you all right?' She looked at me suspiciously. 'If you try to join me at this table, I'll call security,' she said. 'Oh no, not again,' I said, which made a few heads turn our way. I was relieved to see that she was alive, but sloped off back to my seat suspecting that the few people down for breakfast at this hour might get entirely the wrong impression of me if I loitered any longer at Daisy's table.

KATHRINE LEARNS MY WEAKNESS

Walking across the car park to the riverside path, I saw Kathrine throwing something into the water. It was about the size of a cat. When she saw me, she froze. 'That wasn't a cat,' she said. 'I never thought it was,' I said. We sat at a picnic table. From my pocket, I took out several small pastries I had stolen from the breakfast buffet so that I wouldn't have to buy lunch. 'I had a difficult night,' I said. She watched me eat three of the pastries. 'Are we in a workshop?' she said. 'No,' I said. 'Oh,' she said, 'I brought my pen.' A raggedy ruffian of a boy skipped up to us carrying a wicker basket. 'Want to buy a gift for the mister?' he said to Kathrine. 'No,' she said. 'Oh, go on,' I said. 'Yea go on,' the little scruff repeated. 'What are they?' she asked. 'They're surprises, lady. Go on, surprise the mister.' 'Yes, surprise me,' I said, clapping my hands. Kathrine gave the scoundrel a £5 note expecting change. He handed her a present covered in red paper decorated with green sprigs of holly. I pricked my fingers as I began to unwrap it. The little rascal skipped off into the car park, and then on into town. Kathrine stared at the tube of Pringles revealed as the present she had bought me. 'Must I have one?' she said. 'I don't know,' I said, sucking my bloody fingers, 'probably.' 'Then no, I won't,' she said. I put a few Pringles inside a mini cinnamon twist and took a bite. 'Are you going to ask my permission to appear in any of your future work?' Kathrine said. 'Should I?' I said with a mouthful of food. 'It would be polite,' she said. 'Then no, I won't,' I said.

GREEN ROOM

I don't know why, but before I returned to my room it hit me that at some point during the previous evening I had rashly agreed to audition for my friend Yasmina's new production of King Lear. I'm no leading man, and neither am I as young as I once was, so the Fool is the perfect role for me. At least, that's how I convinced myself to accept it when she offered it to me. 'We'll be in touch,' she said after the audition. 'That's great,' I said. 'When do rehearsals start?' But she had already left. Now I come to think of it, I haven't been on stage for thirty years, and I'm petrified I won't be able to learn the lines. I'm so worried that, as I passed a large pot in the lobby, I had to let go a small amount of vomit into the compost surrounding the base of a lovely variegated snake plant. I straightened myself. 'I don't think anybody saw you.' I looked behind me. Two young boys wearing the uniforms of Scouts were crouching down. 'I think you got away with it,' the second boy said. 'We have dreams like that, too,' the first boy said. 'You do?' I asked rather too plaintively. They looked at each other with a creeping contempt for me. 'How do they end?' I said. 'They never end, you fool,' the first said. They both giggled. 'Except in death,' the second said, as if completing an old Music Hall routine. 'Will I survive?' I said. 'How long is the run?' the first said. 'We open in Swindon for a week, and then go out on tour for two months.' 'You won't make the opening night,' the second said. 'Would you like us to clean your car?' the first said. They had been so helpful that I didn't want to tell them I had no car. 'Yes, please' I said. 'Which one is it?' the second said. 'Um, it's the red Ford Fiesta,' I said. They picked up their buckets and sponges and zigzagged out through the lobby, being careful to keep behind each plant pot and comfy chair that lined the route.

BREAK OUT

It was barely an hour since breakfast and already I'd seen enough to know that love was a missing delegate, lost somewhere out there on the motorway. Lost love has neither a map nor a mobile phone. There's no way of knowing when it will arrive, nor if we'll recognise it when it does. We could both check-in at the same time, take adjoining rooms on the eighth floor, ring Reception to order special services after midnight, take our dogs for a walk in the same city centre park, and never so much as nod a silent 'Good Morning' to each other. The lack of such Dickensian coincidences would have tickled us, for sure, during our undergraduate years when reading was never pleasurable, merely a means of displaying our skill at citing literary sources with an accurate bibliographical reference. I was exhausted. Luckily, I overheard a small group of people who had just flown in from Qatar say there were six breakout rooms in the south wing of the Ground Floor. I asked one of them which way was south. He looked at my name tag. 'Well, Tom, that all depends on which way is north, doesn't it?' Such binary choices are how I got into this mess in the first place, but I decided not to share this with him. 'Search for lichen, Tom. Search for lichen.' I knew at that moment I would never find the breakout rooms.

HELPLESS AND AFRAID

There was nobody on the desk. A distressed young woman was trying to get somebody's attention. 'I want to check-in', she said quietly and repeatedly to herself. She began to sway backwards and forwards, then from side to side. Her rocking began to make me a little giddy. 'Why don't you help her?' the man beside me said. He had a silk handkerchief in the top pocket of his suit jacket. 'Why don't you?' I said. We both stood as still as can be while this unnerving spectacle unfolded before us. We were so still, that when the young woman turned to us for support, she couldn't see us. We had become invisible.

THE SOUTH WING

'We hear you've been looking for the breakout rooms.' For a second, that voice sounded like my father's, and made me swallow my chewing gum. 'We?' I said. 'We've been looking forward to hearing your work. It's caused quite a stir.' The tallest of the group looked at my 'Tom' name badge. I had doodled on it. 'Does that say 'Somme'?' Two or three of them seemed impressed by my new name. 'Work?' I said. 'Everybody's here to work, Somme. Without work, we have no purpose. Who sent you?' My breath became short and my chest began to tighten. 'Was it the Senate?' He was persistent, I'll give him that. 'I'm saying nothing,' I said. He and his six friends began to laugh and a few of them slapped me on the back. 'Come on,' they said, 'we'll show you to the south wing.' 'I've changed my mind,' I said, turning to go. A short woman grabbed my arm. She was disturbingly strong. 'Nonsense,' she said, 'you'll love it.' 'I no longer want to go to the south wing,' I spat at them. 'It has become my red line. I will die on this hill.' She pulled me into their legion and we marched southward. 'Oh, Somme,' she said, 'that's a riot. We love you so much!' The click of their feet echoed across the high-domed lobby, a trace of pickaxe-in-a-diamond-mine in its tinny refrain. One of my new accomplices began to whistle 'Heigh-Ho' as people parted before us. 'I wonder if this is how it begins,' I thought. 'When the mask of civility slips, the rule of law, freedom of the press. Like this, skipping lightly to the south wing, with Disney in our hearts.'

HERZLICHE VEREINBARUNG

My captors and I tumbled out of the lift on the 11th floor. Cock-eyed and reeling, they began a raucous and ribald version of 'Bare Necessities'. In their musical excitements, they momentarily took their eyes off me. It proved long enough to dash into Room 1134 and hold my breath until they were gone. I decided to jettison my name tag in an effort to evade recapture should our paths cross again. I unclipped it and threw it onto the end of the first of two twin beds. That's when I saw Herr Gerhard und Frau Frauke Schneider who were naturally very alarmed to see me. I tried to put them at ease with a cheery 'Guten Tag' and go on my way, but Frau Schneider struck me across the forehead with a recently boiled kettle. 'I'm sorry for the intrusion,' I said. 'My room must be next door.' Herr Schneider helped me to my feet and handed me my tag. 'I was looking forward to having dinner with you,' he said, 'but perhaps you should just leave and we shall never speak of this again.' His English was perfect.

THANK YOU, JOHNNY FIVE SPICE

People were streaming out of Conference 6 muttering politely but looking indifferent. Just when it looked like there was nobody else, a middle-aged man staggered out. His scarf had unravelled and was hanging down almost to his foot. He stopped to pick it up but dropped his tote bag. 'Are you all right?' I said, picking it up for him. 'Thank you,' he looked at my latest name tag, 'Johnny Five Spice.' I sneaked a look at his name tag. 'Heavy night, Benedict?' He straightened his scarf and motioned for me to sit cross-legged on the floor. He took a candle from his tote bag and lit it, placing it between us. 'I was sat on a wall with Brad Pitt, I think. It was certainly somebody famous. And it was certainly a man.' He warmed his hands on the candle. 'We were about ten, sitting on a west-facing wall of Clarence Park

firing dried peas at passers-by with our Sekiden guns. They looked like the James Bond Walther PPK. We got them for Christmas. One elderly gentleman was so furious he stopped and demanded we hand them over. Brad was much more middle class than me and afraid of getting into trouble, so he gave his gun to the man. I remember he did it silently, like a black and white slow-motion replay. I told the old fucker to piss off and ran away. "Why do celebrities haunt our dreams like this?" I cried, but I was running so fast nobody could hear me.'
We sat for a while, until Benedict rubbed his tummy. 'I'm hungry,' he said, and got up and walked away. 'What about your stuff?' I called after him. He just waved and walked on, so I snuffed out the candle. Benedict's nostalgic melancholy was contagious. I searched his tote bag, found his pills, and took one more than the recommended dose.

MARRIAGE GUIDANCE

'My wife doesn't understand me.' 'That's an old one.' 'No, really. She's Korean. Her English is non-existent.' 'How did you court one another?' 'We hired a translator. She was a very hardworking translator. Once we were married, the translator moved into the spare room. It was much cheaper. Before, she had to travel across town every day, and wouldn't be able to leave until we had fallen asleep.' 'What happened to her?' 'My wife fired her.' 'Why?' 'She wouldn't say.' 'It might have been jealousy.' 'What makes you say that?' 'It's a common motive. Was she young?' 'Very young. And beautiful.' 'There you have it. It must have been jealousy.' 'Well, now I come to think of it, I suppose I gave her every motive to be jealous.' 'How?' 'We had a long passionate affair. Since well before I met my Korean wife. And it continued after she was fired.' 'Is it still going on?' 'Only Fridays to Mondays.' 'Maybe marriage isn't for you.' 'No?' 'It usually requires a greater degree of commitment than you are willing to give it.' 'You might be right. I can't think why I haven't thought of that before. Thanks, Johnny Five Spice.'

NOTES ON THE DINOSAUR

I settled in the Piano Bar with my lecture notes. 'Is anybody sitting here?' a tall elderly man said. He carried a battered leather satchel that no longer fastened. He joined me on the next stool. 'I recommend the oysters, my friend. Thick and delicious.' I gestured to my name tag. 'Please, call me Johnny. Johnny Five Spice.' He pulled a newspaper from his satchel and opened it extravagantly. 'I would, but that's not your name, is it?' I think my face turned yellow. Or green. I hadn't a mirror. A young woman approached us. 'Good evening, Mr Jalapeño,' she said. She had jet black hair, pale foundation, scarlet lipstick, and a gold ring that pierced her septum. 'A dozen of your finest oysters please, Viscera,' he said. 'And a glass of chilled Chablis Grand Cru, if you don't mind.' Viscera wrote nothing down. She turned to me. I hadn't looked at the menu. 'Give him the panino.' He looked me up and down. 'No garlic.' Viscera left. 'It's on me,' he said, patting my forearm. I unclipped my tag, replaced it with another, and decided to go on the offensive. 'Mr Jalapeño. That's not your name, is it?' I said. He put on his glasses and read my new tag. 'No, Jolene. You're right. It's Jeff.' We sat listening to the pianist play a medley of Billy Joel songs. Viscera returned with our food. She leaned on the counter. Mr Jalapeño slurped his oysters. After the fifth, he examined his wine. 'We were disappointed to miss your paper last night, Jolene,' he said, holding the glass up to the light. I began to sweat. 'You know, the soil from which Chablis rises dates from the Jurassic and Cretaceous ages.' He drank. I picked up my notes and began to edge away. Viscera put half an oyster into her mouth, leaned forward and fed it to Mr Jalapeño. 'There are dinosaurs in this glass, Jolene,' he said.

NO MUSTARD

I thought I had given him the slip but the man with the silk handkerchief was tenacious. We had gone outside to admire the way daylight turned the great river the colour of molten silver, but I quickly grew tired of his conversation. I asked him to nip over to a dirty van at the edge of the car park to buy me a hot dog. When he was out of sight, I ran back to the hotel and hid behind a trolley stacked high with suitcases. Within seconds, like Road Runner, he was standing next to me. 'It's a bit cold now,' he said, handing me the hot dog. 'Where's the sweet yellow American mustard?' I said. He looked crestfallen. 'Are you married?' he said. 'Aren't we all?' I said. 'I'm not,' he said. 'We're all married to something,' I said. 'I can't make up my mind whether women are mythical beings worthy of my worship, or dangerous witches out to manipulate me with their seductive beauty,' he said. I lowered my eyes and shook my head. 'Would you like me to get you that mustard?' he said. I nodded. 'I bet you're married to your job, aren't you?' I said. 'I sell wallpaper,' he said, and went out to the car park to juice up my hot dog.

TIPS

I found Benedict at a stool in the Piano Bar. He was morose. 'You're not supposed to die in dreams, but they don't tell you how close to death you can come,' he said. I tried to cheer him up. 'Close enough to feel fear, probably. And searing panic,' I said. 'I guess that's something we'll never know. Unless there's an afterlife,' he said, and took a sip of kirsch. 'Is there an afterlife?' I said. 'Of course not. Don't be ridiculous,' he downed his kirsch. 'Imagine if there was. We'd never talk about anything else.' Benedict took my kirsch and downed that too. 'Are you giving a paper this afternoon?' he said. 'No,' I said. 'I can't remember.' I said. 'Maybe,' I said. 'I am,' he said, and then asked the barman for more kirsch. 'We should think about a spot of lunch. You can help me with my revisions.' I began to sweat. I felt palpitations high in my chest. 'I don't have a pen,' I said. He scowled. 'After all I've done for you,' he said, sliding off his stool. 'I shall be in the rose garden. Bring sandwiches. No second chances.' As Benedict left, the barman placed two kirsches down in front of me. 'You're a middle child, aren't you?' 'That's astonishing,' I said. 'Worth a tip?' he said. I searched my pockets but had nothing. 'Nobody carries cash anymore,' he said. 'Damn you. Damn you all.'

A TRIP TO THE RUINS

There was a commotion in the lobby. Dozens of people were grabbing packed lunches from the front desk and making their way to the entrance where a rickety old bus idled, gushing its soupy diesel fumes into the atmosphere. A sprightly woman in a tan-coloured two-piece reminded the crowd to wear hard hats. Everybody murmured agreements and thanked her. She had an air of authority, but nobody could find the hard hats. She didn't have one herself, and with this discovery she retreated to the back of the queue and looked at her feet. I grabbed one of the lunches and joined the middle of the queue which, to my surprise, nobody minded. They were too busy checking their silver packages. Some tutted, others shook their heads sadly. A man named Mort was going around collecting unwanted dill pickle slices. 'Boy oh boy, I love these!' he said to anybody who would listen. He had brought spare Tupperware for just this eventuality. Something tugged my sleeve. I looked down and saw two little girls dressed identically, but sucking different coloured lollipops. 'We've never been to the Ruins,' they said in unison. Their mother turned around. 'Your twins are beautiful,' I said. 'What are their names?' 'Alice,' she said. 'What, both of them?' I said. Their father turned around. 'We ran out of ideas.' 'Eugh, this is a piece of shit!' one of the Alices said when she saw the contents of her lunch. 'Now Alice, that's no way to talk,' the other Alice said. 'Fuck off Alice, you stupid cow,' the first Alice said. 'Girls!' the mother said. 'What kind of fucking shithole is this, anyway?' the first Alice said. The father sighed. 'This is why we never get to see the Ruins,' he said, handing me their tickets. 'I hope you can find some use for these,' he said, leading his family to the elevators.

SOMETHING, FEAR PERHAPS

On the bus to the Ruins I had four seats and five lunches to myself. Nearby passengers were jealous and prodded each other, but I was troubled and couldn't enjoy my Schadenfreude. I kept thinking I was expected elsewhere, that people were relying on me to do something, provide something, be somebody. I opened one of the packed lunches and forgot all about it. I began to see why Mort loved dill pickle. It's both sweet and sour at the same time. Before I knew it, I was being shaken awake by a man in a kilt. 'Are you ok?' he said, moving the packed lunch debris and sitting down next to me. 'What?' I said, still groggy. 'You were making threats,' he said. 'You mentioned dunking, foot-roasting, and the shinbone crusher. Some of the older passengers were getting distressed.' He was very kindly. 'Was it a nightmare?' he said. 'I think so,' I said. 'Yes, it must have been. I've never threatened anybody in my life.' He looked at my name tag. 'You have now, Jolene.' He took one of my many small wax-covered cheeses and began to unwrap it. 'The last time something like that happened to me, I dreamt I was in a milk bar with Marlon Brando,' he said. 'We were listening to rock and roll music on the jukebox. A man approached us and shot me square in the head.' I wanted my cheese back, but he put the whole thing in his mouth. 'I felt no pain, nothing, but the look on Marlon's face when he saw my wound was terrifying.' He rested his head on my shoulder. 'Sleep is so damn difficult, isn't it?' he said. I wanted to tell him to eat less cheese, but I was too tired. Before we fell asleep in each other's arms, we watched the city slowly run out of its breathtaking bluster until there was nothing but the vanity of trees.

THE MAN WHO WOULD NOT SHUDDER

I was sheltering from the rain in the charnel house of the Ruins, when a red-cheeked gentleman huffed and puffed his way in to join me. He too had no umbrella. 'Bloody midges,' he said. 'I was told there aren't any in these parts.' He tried to roll up his trouser legs but they were too narrow. He huffed again, undid his belt, clasp and zipper, and dropped his sodden trousers. There were two large circular rings on his left leg: one on his calf and one on the inside of his knee. On his right, there was a similar ring on the front lower part of his thigh. All three rings contained a crimson centre, like a vivid bullseye. 'My oh my,' I said. He wiped his forehead and rubbed his neck. 'How does anybody survive summer in this country?' he said. I was hoping that now he had shown me the problem, he would pull up his trousers, but he just stood there, swelling with pain. 'Have you been for a walk in the country?' I said. 'Yes,' he said. 'While wearing a pair of shorts?' He sat on the stone floor. 'Yes. That's uncanny. Are you some kind of crank?' He lay down slowly. 'I don't have any money, you know.' 'You need to see a doctor,' I said. He was on his back, trousers around his ankles, breathing heavily. He closed his eyes. 'I am a fucking doctor,' he said. 'No, a medical doctor. Those aren't midge bites,' I said. 'Here we go. Project Fear. Doom, doom, doom. I suppose if I don't get treated with antibiotics, I might become severely ill?' The light was fading. 'Yes,' I said. 'Oh do me a favour, Gandhi,' he said, reaching out through the slats of wood to his right. 'Are these real skulls and bones?' he said, stroking a femur. I felt dry enough to return to the surface. 'Yes,' I said. 'Shall I tell the coach driver to wait for you?' But he was snoring. He looked peaceful.

V

I went outside and hailed a taxi. 'I need coffee and free WiFi,' I said to the driver. 'I know just the place,' he said. Within minutes, we were there. 'May I join you?' the driver said. 'No,' I said. 'Right, that'll be a hundred and forty-eight quid, please,' he said. 'What!' I said, and one of my shirt buttons popped open. He peered at me through the rear-view mirror. I did my button up. 'Ok,' I said, 'You can come in, but I'm here to think, so I'd prefer it if you didn't speak to me.' We went inside and I ordered a regular black coffee. 'What do you want?' I said. 'Three Massive Meals please, all with extra fries and chocolate milk shakes,' he announced to the serving boy. He turned to me and said, 'You go and sit down, get on with your thinking. I'll bring everything over.' I took a seat next to the window overlooking the railway line and opened my phone. There was a text: 'wont make yr ppr tonite soz. broke foot on cobbler. bbcnews says watch out fake taxis about. v'. My driver was still in the waiting area. The distance from my seat to the door must have been eight or nine metres, but if I went that way, I would virtually brush his back with my fingernails. A slightly longer route went behind some bench seats filled with noisy families. I grabbed a paper hat and some crayons and wandered out as inconspicuously as I could. A coach drew up. Eighteen cheerleaders got out and went into the burger bar. I waited for their driver to turn his back and jumped aboard. I found a couple of seats about half-way down being used to store gym bags and hid myself under them. The nausea of sleep filled my lungs. I vowed never to frequent multinational fast food outlets again.

OPENING NIGHT

'I can see my master raving in the rain. When he threatens to become naked, we'll make for the hovel and rail against injustice.' 'Say what?' a young woman says. 'Make no noise,' I say. 'Excuse me?' she says, with a trace of Californian. 'I'll go to bed at noon,' I say. 'I beg your pardon?' she says, agitated. 'Endeavour thyself to sleep, and leave thy vain bibble babble!' With no more ado, she picks up a stick and begins to strike me about the arms and back. As I race from my hiding place under a pile of gym bags, the driver of the coach brakes sharply, throwing me down the aisle and onto the floor by the double doors. 'Open them, I beg you,' I say to him. But he reaches for his mobile phone and dials the police. Cheerleaders are picking themselves off the floor and advancing toward me. They have batons and ropes. The doors suddenly open and Kathrine is outside standing next to the emergency button. 'Quick!' she says. I run down the stairs, grab her by the hand, and we head west. 'You're in the wrong play, Mark,' she says. 'Nay, I'll ne'er believe a madman till I see his brains,' I say as we reach a station of the metro. 'I will fetch you light and paper and ink,' Kathrine says. 'Atta girl,' I say, and we jump the next train to Finnieston. The late Jessica Albrighton sits opposite us. 'One of the delights of sleep is the freedom it offers,' she says. 'No matter where we are, sleep allows us to roam elsewhere.' We nod, though I suspect Kathrine doesn't believe her. 'You should have seen my Olivia. I was the talk of the South Bank.' We are sure she is lying, but somehow moved by the solemnity of her performance. 'You are my favourite actress, Miss Albrighton,' I say, and she hugs herself with such delight that I suspect she is not dead, as reported in 1983, but very much alive and planning a comeback.

EXPLAINING JOKES TO RONNIE

It was a relief to be back inside the hotel. I went to Reception and asked for Daisy. 'Daisy doesn't work here anymore,' a gruff middle-aged man with a Birmingham accent said. I looked at his badge. 'What happened, Ronnie?' Ronnie shrugged his shoulders. 'Hand in the till? Flippin Chickens?' he said. 'Did she say anything about my paper?' I said. He opened a drawer and took out some safe deposit box keys. 'Name?' I was still wearing my 'Jolene' name tag, so I poked around in my pocket, found a new one and switched them. 'Dr Benson Casablanca,' I said. Ronnie frowned. He skimmed some envelopes and took one out. 'Sign here,' he said. 'Is there a programme of events?' I said. Ronnie handed me a booklet headed 'Medicine & the Philosophy of Tomorrow'. The vast number of delegates in the hotel began to make sense. 'How many different conferences are here this weekend?' I said, handing it back to him. 'You ask a lotta questions, punk,' Ronnie said. 'Some kinda wiseguy, hunh?' He had assumed the accent of Manhattan's Lower East Side. 'No,' I said. 'Humanities. I'm giving a paper,' I said. 'Want me to get Fat Tony to tell ya?' My mouth went dry. I couldn't speak. 'Mad Millie McVie? Vinny Big Ears Gambini? Jimmy The Golf Ball?' I shook my head. 'Just a conference schedule,' I said, hoarsely. I saw a pile on the desk. 'Oh, here they are.' I took one and backed away, keeping him in my sightline. 'You get a little hungry, I know a good clam house on Mulberry,' he said. 'Ask for Allesandro. Tell him Carmine sent ya.' The phone rang and he was distracted. I slipped Dr Casablanca back into my pocket and buffed up my Jolene. It was a relief to return once more to the safety of Country music.

BOB-A-JOB WEEK

I was on my way outside to get some air when a man collapsed at my feet. A flame-haired young woman emerged from behind a portable retractable banner stand. 'What have you done?' she said, twisting my arm behind my back. 'This is a ludicrous mistake,' I said. She kicked me in the back of the knee and I went down. The man got to his feet and checked to see if anybody was watching. The place was deserted. He seized me by the collar and pulled me to my feet. 'Hand over the name tag, Jolene.' With my free hand, I unclipped my tag and held it out to him. 'I'll have that,' the flame-haired woman grabbed it. 'Please don't take it,' her partner began. Her eyes narrowed. 'Don't say it,' she said. He swallowed. 'Just because you can,' he finished. 'I warned you,' she said, and mumbled something into her sleeve. Three armed men ran in and forced him to his knees, his arms behind his head. 'Are you all right sir,' one of them said to me, helping me up. 'Yes, yes, thank you,' I said. 'Sir, you should look away now,' another said. 'Why?' I said. He raised his pistol and shot the man in the back of the head. The shooter closed my hand and fingers around the grip and trigger of his gun, and they ran away. As I slipped the gun into my pocket, the two Scouts stomped toward me. 'There were twelve red Ford Fiestas in the car park. You owe us £180,' one of them said. 'What?' I said. 'We cleaned all of them,' the other said. 'Cash,' the first one said. I pulled out the gun. 'What a laughably crude reproduction,' the first said. 'Come on, give us the money,' the second said. I pulled the trigger. The bullet blew the second Scout's entire head off his shoulders. 'I don't have any cash,' I said. 'That is so cool,' the first Scout said, reaching for the gun. I wiped it clean on my sleeve and handed it to him. 'Be careful,' I said, 'it's definitely loaded.'

AU SECOURS!

I was scoffing hot smoked salmon on toasted sourdough bread when a couple joined me. I glanced at their name tags. Dr Antonin took out a cigarette and lighter. Professor Claudette DeClercq reminded him that smoking indoors was no longer permitted. Claudette sipped her soup. 'Putain,' she cursed, spitting it back in the bowl. Distracted, Antonin looked at my new name tag. 'And what is your subject, Dr Wendy Potemkin?' he said. I was momentarily unsure. 'Let me guess,' he said. 'You are an historian?' he said. 'Yes, of course, that's it,' I said. 'I am eating the runny shit from a horse's arse,' Claudette said. A couple of waiters gave the impression they might come over to our table and ask if we had any problems, but then went back to their duties. 'And what does History teach us, Wendy?'

Antonin said, sniffing Claudette's soup. 'Ça pue la merde,' he whispered in agreement with her. 'Well, it tells us everything, Antonin,' I said, thinking that if I kept it simple, I might not be revealed as Not-An-Historian, and be able to finish my salmon. 'I will tell you what History does, Dr Wendy Potemkin,' Claudette said. 'History reveals the paucity of our forethought.' Claudette pushed the bowl away from her and some of it splashed in my lap. They got up to go. 'We are looking forward to your paper, Dr Potemkin,' Claudette said without pausing to register my surprise and alarm. 'Allez, Antonin.' Before following her, he quickly checked she wasn't watching and handed me a napkin. He had written something on it. His brow was wet with sweat. I held the napkin up to the light, but I don't speak French, or any language other than English, so I mopped up the soup in my lap and finished my salmon.

MY MOST MALE OF LOVERS

When my best friend Kipling died, everybody was surprised when I said I wasn't going to the funeral. 'So what was the last thing Kipling said to you?' one of my old friends said. 'I don't really remember,' I said. 'I mean, I've made something up in the event that I am asked what was the last thing he said to me. It offers everybody a crumb of comfort. Even me.' My old friend asked me what was the thing that I had invented as Kipling's last words to me. 'I love you, Mark,' I said. 'That's lovely,' my old friend said. 'Yes,' I said. 'If only it was remotely the kind of thing he might have said to me on our last meeting.' 'Oh dear,' my old friend said, 'did it not end well between you?' 'Not really,' I said. 'So much so, it's hard to be truly upset at his passing. He pulled out of our friendship like a lackadaisical lover who knows you're not on the pill but doesn't care awfully much whether you end up pregnant.' My old friend seemed unsettled that I was talking about Kipling this way. 'In fact,' I pressed on, 'he'd be the kind of lover who would be quietly pleased to have a bastard child because he would see it as proof and triumph that he had sex just once in his lonely life with a sentient human being.' A man in the booth next to me leaned over the top and looked around. 'Who are you talking to?' he said. 'Nobody,' I said, removing my 'Wendy' name tag from my breast and placing her in a bowl of cold gazpacho. 'Did you really have a friend called Kipling?' he said. 'Apparently not,' I said.

THE SIDORSKY PASS

I followed the sound of laughter coming from the men's changing rooms in the Leisure Area. It was filled with treadmills, rowing machines, weightlifting benches, sweating bodies, and pop music. It wasn't at all leisurely. A young woman in a loose cinnamon-coloured suit offered me a bath towel and 10ml tube of body lotion. 'What's this for?' I said, but she just smiled. A fitness instructor was taking some old age pensioners through a moderately physical routine. During a rest period, she approached me. 'This group is doing one more rep, and then I'm moving on to a more advanced class, if you're interested,' she said. 'We'll be doing The Sidorsky Pass.' 'That sounds exciting,' I said, 'but I was going to check out the men's changing rooms.' 'Why?' she said. 'It sounds like they're having so much fun,' I said. She looked at me gravely. 'These things are never what they seem,' she said. 'They aren't?' She glanced to the door and lowered her volume. 'It's true what they say, you know,' she said. 'About what?' I said. 'Politics.' I must have looked confused. 'Tragedy is easy. It's Politics that's difficult. I'm really a choreographer with the City Ballet. I know what I'm talking about.' She handed me a card. It read 'Florence Sidorsky: Choreographer'. 'It's a small class. Room 1239. I'll be there in ten minutes. Go and warm up.' It was so busy nobody saw me sneak out without returning the towel and lotion. Though this felt like a little victory, I was soon crushed by anxiety. 'Are you all right?' a passing hotel employee said. 'I don't like making decisions,' I said. 'I can't tell you what to do,' she said, 'but what I can say is that all my dreams begin and end on the 12th floor.' I found this so edifying I needed to take a selfie with her, but my phone wouldn't work. She took it from me to inspect. 'This is a piece of shit,' she said, and went on her way.

ROOM 1239

The door to each room on 12th displayed a sign designating its activity: 1235 'Fire-eating'; 1237 'Hacking Facebook'; 1239 'The Sidorsky Pass'. I knocked. A couple greeted me. 'Good morning. I am Hela, devoted foe of Thor, Asgardian goddess of death,' one of them said. 'Hello,' I said. 'Good morning. I am Thor, son of Odin, crown prince of Asgard, god of thunder, lightning, and fertility. Relentless slayer of my numerous enemies. You won't be needing this,' the other said, taking my tube of lotion and throwing it into a plastic bucket filled with tubes of lotion. 'No working projectile weapons, paddles, clubs, metal bats, ice skates?' Hela waited for a response. I shook my head. 'Revealing costumes are not a sign of consent, so no touching the players.' I nodded. 'Naked flames, smoke bombs, crowbars, chainsaws?' 'No,' I said. 'Mace?

Pepper spray?' Thor motioned for me to go through to the bedroom. 'Make yourself comfortable,' he said. 'The Repair Station is on the 10th floor.' I lay down, but began to panic about the Repair Station. 'Repair Station!' I shouted. Thor entered. 'You haven't even put on your costume,' he said. 'This isn't the Humanities conference, is it?' I said. 'This is the 12th floor. We're anything you want us to be,' Hela said, lowering her antlers into my face. 'I've changed my mind,' I said, and hurried out of the room. There was a long queue for yoga outside 1241. Excitement filled the corridor, except for one man who shifted from foot to foot. 'I'll swap you this towel for that mat,' I said. 'Oh, thank you,' he said, snatching my towel and running toward the stairwell. Somebody stepped out and tripped him. Two more pulled him back into line. 'Be strong, Terry,' another said. Terry struggled but soon lost strength. 'Oh well,' I said to the people nearest me as I was leaving. 'Have some nice yoga.'

WHO IS MR GRANDHOMME?

I was worried about not getting enough exercise, so decided to take the stairs. As I reached the 6th floor, I thought I heard the sound of protestors and peeked through the door. A crowd had gathered outside Conference Room Eight. They squinted angrily at anybody trying to enter and chanted, 'No voice for Mr Grandhomme!' 'Who's Mr Grandhomme?' I said to a couple of security guards. 'He's been barred from speaking via tele-link from Moscow,' one of them said. 'Zoom. Florida,' the other said. 'Florida,' the first repeated. 'Zoom.' Some protestors overheard us. 'He's been smuggled into the building! He's in there now!' Three protesters tried to barge their way in but were no match for hotel security. 'He's sitting at the top table about to speak!' one said. 'No voice for Mr Grandhomme!' they cried as one. 'Wait!' one of them pointed at me. 'That's him.' The pointing protestor was unshaven, about six foot three, with a scar running from just below his right eye to the corner of his mouth. 'That's Mr Grandhomme!' The elevator pinged and I began to make my way to its doors. The protesters started to follow me. The security guards made no move to protect me. I glanced down at my chest to check I hadn't inadvertently pinned the 'Mr Grandhomme' name tag to my shirt. I hadn't. This was my chance. 'Look,' I said tugging at my new tag. 'My name is Max Samuels.' They froze. Slowly, they began to turn on the man with the scar. 'Maybe he's Mr Grandhomme,' one of them said. 'Yea,' another agreed. The man with the scar began to disappear from view beneath the mob. Life can be cheap, I thought, checking my pockets. I was running out of name tags. I wouldn't last a second day at this rate.

VERTIGO

I sat with a newspaper and spied on Reception for twenty minutes to make sure Ronnie was off duty. Eventually, I was sure he must have gone home, and approached the desk. I looked at the Receptionist's name tag. 'Hi Francine, I'd like to change rooms. I want a room on a lower floor. The lowest floor possible, please.' She opened her computer. 'I'm afraid we are fully booked this weekend. As you can see, we have several conferences going on. People from all over the world are here.' 'Yes, I can see that,' I said. 'But the higher I go, the stranger everything becomes. I'm scared.' She clicked her mouse. 'As I say,' she looked at my name tag, 'Mr Samuels, there are no unoccupied rooms anywhere in the building.' 'Do you have any idea what's going on in this building?' I said, getting a little frantic. 'Actually, yes,' she said, turning the screen toward me. 'All the events are listed here, look.' I did look. 'What the hell is happening on the 23rd Floor?' I said. She quickly turned the screen back. 'Woops,' she said. 'Woops?' I said. She closed her browser. 'I'm sorry. Some information is restricted.' 'This isn't good enough,' I said. 'Do you need something to calm you down? Would you like me to call you a doctor?' she said. 'Is that supposed to be funny?' I said. Somebody was checking in at the next computer terminal. 'Come on, be fair. That was funny,' she said. I looked at her tag. 'I don't recall asking for your opinion, Dr White.' Somebody else was checking in to our left. 'There's no need to be rude,' she said. 'I don't recall asking you either,' I looked at her tag, 'Dr Wong.' The three of them sniggered. 'You're a real bunch of comedians,' I said. The two Doctors high-fived and made their way to the elevators. 'Come on,' Francine said. 'Lighten up, it's going to be a long weekend.'

CASH FLOW PROBLEMS

A crowd had gathered outside the revolving doors on a patch of grass near the water fountain. A small woman was crouched over a display of cards and irregularly shaped white stones. Next to her was a hat in which people had tossed coins. 'What is the saddest song you've ever heard? The saddest sight you've ever seen?' She paused and picked up the hat. One or two people threw more coins. 'What is the saddest book you've ever read? Did it feel like lemons in a wound, or did it feel like boulders on your chest?' She shook the hat this time. A couple moved away, intent on finding a quieter place to talk. 'What is the saddest dream you've ever dreamed? Is it this one?' Several people began to shift uneasily from side to side. Four or five turned and left. 'Is it the one where everybody you love is sitting with you in the same room, eating crisps and passing round the hummus, half-watching the tv because you're more interested in each other, your lives, your hard days, all of you in shorts and t-shirts, just an inch or so out of reach, unable to touch?' The crowd was gone. She reached into the hat and drew out a handful of coins to count. 'That was very good,' I said. 'I'd like to give you something, but I don't carry cash.' She waved me away. 'Bring me some fruit,' she said. 'But not bananas. I hate bananas. Bananas make me sick.' She took a large purse from her apron and put the money in it with a loud click. 'Ok,' I said, 'I will.' She looked into my eyes and then spat on the floor. 'Liar,' she said, and walked off toward a flat-bottomed barge with cranes.

SHOWER SCENE

I had to clean up. The morning's events had left me feeling dirty. I could no longer remember in which room I was staying, so I followed a frail professor to his suite on the 10th floor and pushed him through the door as he opened it. I blindfolded him with an antimacassar from the armchair and asked him not to make a fuss. He agreed. 'People will buy anything,' he said. 'Everything's for sale. There's always somebody willing to be a middleman. Everybody's happy because everybody's making money.' I asked him to talk a little more softly because I had a headache. 'I can't even give my memories away,' he said. 'I don't need them, I don't want them. They're irrelevant. I'm embarrassed to continually make reference to myself through them.' I rubbed my temples. 'Shhh,' I said. 'If you keep talking, I'm going to have to stuff something in your mouth.' He nodded. 'I'm going to take a shower, and then I'll release you, ok?' He nodded again. 'Just don't use my toothpaste,' he said. 'It's very high in fluoride. Prescription only. You may have a reaction to it.' 'Thank you,' I said. I felt I could trust him. He was a kind old man. 'Is the blindfold too tight?' I said. 'It's fine,' he said. 'In fact, it's rather comfortable.'

CHECK

In a quiet corner of the Bistro a woman without a name badge was playing chess against herself. She motioned for me to sit next to her. She looked at the board the way a crocodile peers above the waterline scanning for prey. Just as I began to get bored, her hand flew out, she shifted a white piece, whacked a clock, picked up her chair and clattered to the other side of the table. 'Come on, come on!' she said, so I followed her. We settled. Minutes passed. I fidgeted. I felt in my pocket for my remaining name badges. 'I bet there's somebody in here who understands chess,' I thought. 'Shh,' she said. 'I have to erase my white mind,' she whispered. 'What?' I said. 'Utterly. Unconditionally. I can't be black until my white mind is gone.' I found a strip of antacid tablets and punched out two from their silver strip. 'I have a touch of indigestion,' I whispered. 'I'm trying to train myself to operate on two conscious levels, separate and incapable of knowing each other,' she whispered. I sucked my tablets. They were minty. 'Why?' I said. 'I don't want to glorify one of my selves at the cost of paying the other self in humiliations,' she said. I thought that was rather silly, and maybe she was punishing one of her selves by not taking delight in the oppression she could execute, the advantages she could take, of her other self. 'That's very honourable,' I said. More minutes passed. Every so often she would note something down in a notebook which she kept on the table to her left. I was about to ask how long a game of chess generally took to complete when her hand shot out, moved a black piece, and whacked the clock. She picked up her chair and scraped it noisily to the other side of the table. 'Come on, come on!' she cried. I followed her. I lacked the bravery to voice my question.

COLD MEATS

I was standing in line for antipasti, cheese, crackers, and cubed watermelon, when four men wearing cowboy boots pushed in front of me. 'Excuse me,' I said, 'there's a queue.' They were busy discussing golf, practising their swings while they talked. One demonstrated a 'slice', another a 'pull', then they all shouted 'Fore!' and laughed like drains. 'Excuse me,' I repeated. One of them turned and looked down at my name badge. 'Say, somebody misspelled your name, Bryan.' 'It's Bryn,' I said, 'and there's a queue here.' At this point I noticed that all of them were six foot five or more, and three times as wide as me. 'What's up?' the second said to the first. 'Bryan here says there's a queue.' The queue was shortening. 'You play golf, Bryan?' the first said as he picked up the whole bowl of mayonnaise from which people were supposed to take a portion each. 'No,' I said. 'We're just gonna finish this snack and take a bus to the nearest course,' the third said. The amount of food on their plates got higher. 'Why don't you join us?' the first said. The bowl of ketchup was next. Then the two choices of mustard. The fourth man picked up all the jugs of fruit juice in one hand. 'Man, this looks good,' he said. As they went to find a table, the people behind me groaned. The buffet was bare. 'I only wanted a slice of Emmental,' one said to me. 'If you had been stronger, there would have been salami for everybody,' another said.

SLEEPING IT OFF

People were shuffling past a body that lay on a table in the snooker room, so I joined them. 'Should we call a doctor?' I asked the young woman in front of me who was chewing gum. 'Shh, have some respect,' she said. I turned to a couple of middle aged men dressed for a ten pin bowling competition. 'What happened?' I said. 'It's been four years,' one of them said. 'We were in this very room the last time the conference was held in this hotel,' the other said. 'We much prefer Glasgow to Leicester,' the first said. 'Or Swansea,' the second said. 'I like Swansea,' the first said. 'But not as much as Glasgow,' the second said. 'Four years ago?' I said. 'Oh yes,' the first said. 'The poor fellow fell asleep. Right there on the table.' I thought I saw the sleeping man open his eyes momentarily. 'All the things he's missed,' one of them said. 'My birthdays, for example,' the other said. 'His own,' the first said. 'Imagine if life was just a succession of birthdays,' the other said. 'Just presents and cake all day long,' the first said. 'But it isn't, is it?' I said. The bowlers sighed. They climbed onto the table and lay down next to the body. 'Shall I get you a blanket?' I said. 'Shh,' the first said. 'Have some respect.' He put his arm around his friend. 'Goodnight Dennis,' he said. Dennis put his thumb in his mouth. 'Goodnight Bob,' he said. 'See you when it's all over.'

THE OLD SILENCES

By lunchtime on the second and only full day, I still had no idea when I was due to speak, what topic my paper was due to be addressing, if I had even written it yet, and if so, how I might find a copy of it. I figured that there must be somebody at one of the three conferences here in the hotel whom I must know, so I went looking for them. I began on the Ground Floor. After checking the bars and eateries, the spa and leisure areas, the shops and corridors, the conference suites, the meeting rooms, the private rooms, and the currency exchange kiosk, I took a right into the kitchens and sat down for a rest. Staff were far too busy to notice me. They clattered chrome pots and pans, rushed about with steaming trays of broth, and waved sharp knives in each other's faces. 'Are you here with one of the conferences?' a voice behind me said. I looked around to find an elderly gentleman in a grey suit quite out of breath and mopping his forehead with a linen napkin. 'I must be,' I said. 'I'm supposed to be giving a paper on my stone,' he said, lifting a kilo bag of coffee beans. 'That's not a stone,' I said. 'It's a long story,' he said, 'and half the weight.' 'How heavy is it supposed to be?' I asked, but was suddenly struck with the boredom of it and didn't want to hear the answer. 'Do you really want to know?' he said, a little surprised by my interest. 'Yes, of course,' I said. 'The stone is the same size and weight as the average human brain,' he said. 'So now you have only half a brain?' 'Something like that,' he said. 'I misplaced the stone when I changed trains at Crewe, and now I have this coffee.' He wanted me to ask him what his paper was about, but I wasn't playing. 'I'm with the Geologists on Epoch-Naming,' he began, but I cut him off. 'It's probably on its way to Carlisle,' I offered by way of comfort. 'Sorry?' he said. 'Your stone.' 'Ah,' he said. We sat for a while.

THE NEW JERSEY CRUMB COFFEE CAKE INCIDENT

I shuffled my papers and rose. 'The subject of my talk today is "The New Jersey Crumb Coffee Cake". Why, colleagues, is there no coffee in the New Jersey Crumb Coffee Cake?' Mutterings from the floor interrupted my concentration. 'This is not the place for discussion of cake!' somebody called out. From across the room an elderly woman who had forgotten to take off her hat raised her hand. 'Oh do sit down you silly little girl,' she said. 'Let us enjoy our cake in peace.' At that moment, a brouhaha erupted toward the back of the room by the table with tea and biscuits. 'You're asking the wrong question!' a man wearing a red baseball cap shouted at me. One of his crowd stood and pointed at him. 'Take a hike, mister! You don't know anything. You're from New

York!' The audience was now fully engaged. 'What a success,' I thought. One of my fellow speakers on the platform shook her head. 'How are we going to follow this?' Another snapped his pencil. 'You could have warned us,' he said. The Chair of the panel stood and the room went silent. 'How does she do that?' the next speaker whispered in awe. 'As you ought to know,' the Chair said, 'the crumb cake is a German invention using yeast, not the abomination of baking powder and bicarbonate of soda. Once again, you Americans have bastardised a perfectly fine European tradition for the sake of the Yankee Dollar.' Everybody sat and looked sheepish. 'Shame on you,' the Chair said with a flourish. A few of us began to whisper it. Then more. Soon, the room was filled with incantation. 'Shame on us,' we said, all of us, in unison, low in pitch, emitting our guilt as one, pushing it out into the room, all for a slice of authentic Streuselkuchen.

TAMBARA SONNENTAG, CRYING

I was in the gift shop with no intention of buying anything when I started to panic. I threw some items onto the counter, paid, and ran to the Bistro next door. I poured the trinkets onto a table and began to breathe in and out of the empty bag. My heart slowed, the palpitations reduced. A tall woman with long ruby red earrings appeared over the top of the booth next to me. She watched as I brought myself under control. I caught a glimpse of her name tag. She smiled at me. 'Would you like to come and hear me give a short paper in a minute? I'm just finishing my tea and biscuits,' she said. 'What's it on?' I said. 'The Multiplications of Men and Power,' she said. 'Fuck, no,' I said. 'Is it too early?' she said. 'Fuck, yea,' I said. 'It's ok, I understand,' she said. Her head sank beneath the booth and I heard her sip her tea. 'Thank you,' I called. She didn't reply, but I could hear her sipping some more. It sounded like she cracked a biscuit, but I couldn't hear her eating it. It's really something to eat that quietly. In my experience, chocolate bourbons are the worst. Chocolate bourbons are so damn loud. And then I heard it. The sound of Tambara Sonnentag, crying. I picked up my gift shop tat, slid out of my booth, and went around to her table. She blew her nose into a napkin and looked up, as if expecting me to have changed my mind and come listen to her speak. I placed a postcard in front of her. 'This is for you.' She looked at it. 'It's the River Clyde,' I said, 'with the Squinty Bridge in the foreground.' She turned it over to see that it was blank. 'But I don't want it,' she said. 'I hope your paper goes well,' I said, and left.

MANHATTANS, MARGARITAS, & MOJITOS

Saturday night in the Roaring Twenties Bar was grooving. My paper had been hijacked by controversy earlier in the day, and I needed to regain some composure. I ordered three different cocktails hoping it might look like I was waiting for some friends. This fancy was short-lived because I drank them very quickly and ordered three different ones. I soon decided I was going to drink every cocktail on the menu. By eight-thirty I was laughing uproariously. When people looked at me, I raised my glass to them. My joyous conviviality brought several conference-goers to the table for brief exchanges, until one bob-haired woman in a 1980s floral midi-dress sat down across from me. I looked at her name tag, which she had hung from a ribbon and tied in her hair. 'Belinda?' I said. She smiled and picked up my Blood and Sand. 'Help yourself,' I said. She threw the straw away and downed it in one. 'I used to have a dog named Belinda,' I said. She held the glass next to her cheek and stared at me. 'She would lick my face when she was excited,' I said. Belinda was very quiet. She put down the glass, picked up the Dark 'n' Stormy, and stirred it. 'Are you trying to flirt with me?' In my own way, I think I was. 'Oh god, no,' I said. She picked up her small clutch bag and mobile phone, and stood. 'I'm going to sit over there,' she said, without pointing anywhere. 'Right you are,' I said, and picked up the cocktail menu. The Amaretto Sour was next.

DIXIE & PEACHES

Somebody said there was karaoke up on 10th, and I was persuaded to follow a group of Sociologists who were hoping to sing Dolly Parton hits. When we got there, the whole floor was decked in 70s chic: rusty brown, creamy brown, a shot of ruddy brown here and there. I'd forgotten how brown the 70s had been. I was surprised to find Kathrine at the Abba table. 'I thought you hated karaoke,' I said. 'I'm waiting for the 80s,' she said, getting out her knitting 'There must be something to look forward to, Mark. Otherwise, we are lost.' I agreed but felt myself about to faint. Two buff male bouncers wearing nothing but tight denim shorts and biker chain caps, propped me up on either side. Their names were cast in glitter on their caps. 'I feel naked without a moustache,' I said to Dixie. The opening bars of 'More, More, More' drifted our way. My boys introduced the 'Oooohs' and the 'How do you like your loves' with such grace and subtlety that I took the microphone. I may have drunk every cocktail in the joint, but tonight I was going to get the action going. A crowd gathered. People swayed. There was grinding. In the horns and keyboard break, it became evident that this was not the radio-friendly three minutes, but the full six-minute dance floor version. 'Peaches, if I don't find a way out of this sweat and sensuality, I may have a heart attack,' I said. 'You sure are sailing with a cargo full of love and devotion,' he said, leading me to some burgundy-coloured leather benches. 'You'll be safe here,' he said, 'but when we stop singing, look behind you. There's nothing more horrifying than silence.'

UP ON THE ROOF

I had drifted into peaceful reverie in the rooftop bar. Midnight's cooling breeze soothed my hot face. Without warning, a cacophony of blades and the searing searchlight beams of a helicopter raged above me. A harness was lowered to the deck near a crowd of people. A rugged man in heavy body armour tried to keep the crowd back. A couple joined me at my table. Their name tags declared them to be Richard and Diego. 'Has somebody been injured?' I said. They nodded. 'There was an argument,' Richard said. He had a flash of red hair. He combed his fingers through it to take it off his face 'They're colleagues. At Durham, I think,' Diego said. He had a full and frenzied beard. It fluttered in the whip of the helicopter wind. The three of us looked over at the ruckus. A man wearing sunglasses pointed at the crowd, shouting at them. 'This is like Die Hard,' Richard said. The rugged man wrestled the shouting man to the ground and the crowd applauded. 'I'll never sleep now,' Diego said. A man's body was being winched aboard the helicopter. A second helicopter flew past, then came back to hover nearby. Its television news crew filmed the whole scene. A young woman speaking into a microphone leant out perilously. It was Kathrine. 'You'd think people would have better things to do,' Richard said. 'I'm going to the room.' Diego got up to join him. He put his hand in Richard's and turned to me. 'Things were so much more civilised before Twitter,' he said.

COME TO THE RIVER

I was in a small room that had been hastily converted into an amusement arcade for the weekend's conferencegoers. I looked through the large plate glass windows that ran along the whole of one wall. It was dark. Beyond sat the lazy river. To my surprise, lit from below by high-powered ground level floodlights, Kathrine waved at me. She beckoned for me to come outside. It was very late, and I didn't have my cardigan, but it was far too tempting to pass up. The windows were locked. I needed to go back through Reception and around the building to where she was standing. As I reached the brightly lit centre of the lobby, my phone pinged. It was a text: 'ill b thr 4 yr ppr 2moro. got crutches. bbc sayz fake kathrines about. b carefl. v.' I looked up. She was now on the other side of the front revolving doors, waving me forward. I walked over to the window next to the doors and leant my hands against the glass. 'I'm scared, Kathrine,' I said. 'Don't be scared,' she said. 'Come to the river.'

THE GOOD STUFF

Sleep is a remote possibility at conference, so I booked a masseuse. 'The Spa's roof is leaking,' said the bright young man on Reception. 'There may be a delay.' He pointed me toward the elevators. 'Arthur has relocated to a suite on the Second Floor.' He handed me a room key card and a discount voucher. I was so delighted to save money that I wasn't paying attention and took a Service elevator by mistake. I was surprised at how many levels there were beneath the Ground Floor. When it reached minus seven, the doors opened. It was humid and smelled of burning farmland. I pressed the button to go up. Nothing happened. I pushed the alarm. Nothing. I figured there must be stairs nearby, so I stepped into the darkness. Pipes hissed, the floor was slippery. A man appeared in front of me. His hair was long and knotted. 'I'm Pablo.' He drank from a bottle of gin, and handed it to me. 'You shouldn't be down here,' he said, leaning on a pipe. The boiling heat had no adverse effect on him. Something began to drip from the ceiling into his hair, then down his forehead. He wiped it with a finger and put it in his mouth. 'Bitchin,' he said. 'I got in the wrong elevator,' I said. The wail of barn owls surrounded us. 'Save it for later,' he said. Rocks began to strike the pipes, hurled at us from out of the gloom. Pablo pulled me to him. 'I told you not to come back here.' We ran. 'I'm giving a paper in the morning,' I said. 'On what?' he said, a little annoyed at my lack of fitness. 'Madness in the Rain: the uses of water in literature from 1387-1953.' 'That's a vast canvas, man,' he said. 'It's my life's work,' I said. He stopped and raised a syringe. 'Do you want to finish it someday?' Before I could answer, he jabbed me full of serum. The last thing I heard was Pablo's assurance: 'It might be cruel to say it bro, but none of this is relevant'.

TRAINS BOUND FOR NOWHERE

I regained consciousness in one of the many hotel restaurants. Two of my fingers were strapped together in a splint. There was a note on the table. 'Polite reminder: guests are not permitted to use the service elevators.' A man polishing his spectacles bumped into my table and rubbed his thigh. I showed him my fingers. 'Good job that's not your writing hand,' he said. 'But it is my writing hand,' I said. 'Damn, I had a fifty-fifty chance, too.' He sat across the table from me. 'Maybe I was in a fight,' I said. 'There are some real troublemakers at these conferences.' He rose quickly to his feet. 'We should go to the Riverboat Casino. It's open all night.' He sounded like he'd undergone an epiphany. 'How much should we bet?' I said. He emptied his pockets. A room key card, thirty-eight pounds and sixty pence, three buttons, and a torn receipt for Chicken

McNuggets®. 'Everything,' he said. 'I like your style,' I said, emptying my own pockets. 'Wow, how many name tags do you have?' He picked up a handful and chose one. 'I want to be Johnny Five Spice. I've heard good things about him.' I scratched my chin. I was convinced I'd off-loaded Johnny earlier that day. He pinned it to his chest. 'Be careful with Johnny,' I said. 'Why?' he said. 'You should never meet your heroes,' I said. 'They are rotten, sour-faced egomaniacs.' His face fell. I thought he might cry. 'My luck has to change,' he said. I put my arm around his shoulder. 'Come on, Johnny. Let's go outside.' He took a step back. 'I think there's somebody out there to whom I owe a debt I can never repay,' he said. I took his hand to console him, but it hurt like hell. 'Other hand,' I said, shaking my broken fingers. 'We're better together, aren't we?' he said. For the first time since we met, I began to mistrust Johnny Five Spice. 'Let's not be rash,' I said. 'Let's see how the dice fall.'

THE CRUELLER IT IS, THE SOONER IT'S OVER

The streetlights across the river were firm, strong, and bright, unlike the dreary, out-of-focus, sickly yellow ones on this side. Johnny Five Spice stopped. 'This isn't a Riverboat Casino,' he said. The place was dark, doors bolted, padlocks on the gate to the boarding jetty. 'My city guide must be out of date.' The sign on the door read, 'Museum of The American Civil War'. 'Who the hell would want to visit a place like this?' I said. Johnny tapped my shoulder and pointed to the river path on our right. A long line of people in sleeping bags and cheap pop-up tents were queueing, sharing stories, passing around battleground antiques. A striking Union kepi hat with chinstrap caught my eye. 'How much do you want for this?' I said. 'A thousand pounds,' the hat's owner said. 'Are you mad?' I said. 'Goodness, perhaps I am. Ok, thirty quid.' 'Bargain,' I said, and gave him the money. Marlon sat down contentedly and counted his money. Johnny Five Spice stamped his feet and marched off. 'Johnny, wait,' I called. The soles of my blistered feet were on fire. I was limping. He turned back. 'That was despicable,' he said. 'That poor man might have children.' I caught up with him. 'Don't be like this, Johnny. It's a really cool hat.' Johnny ripped off his name tag, tearing his casual shirt. 'This,' he waved it in my face. He grabbed my hat. 'And this!' He threw them both into the water. 'We've been through so much together and I don't even know your name,' I said. There were several splashes behind us. The Museumgoers were diving into the river. 'Give me another tag,' he said. 'Pot luck?' He nodded. I fished out a name from the collection in my pocket. He looked delighted. I pinned it to the undamaged part of his shirt. 'Hello, Meredith.' We held hands and made our way back to the hotel. 'I feel lucky,' he said.

PETTING ZOO

I had signed up for the ukulele class in the Ballroom. There was a crowd of us waiting for the instructor. 'Do you know what I find gratifying?' a middle-aged man with a tank top a size too small for him said. 'We've been here since late Friday afternoon and I haven't heard a single person refer to their pets. I'm definitely enrolling in next year's conference.' 'What are pets?' said a man wearing a cape. A confused hush descended. A passing waiter whispered in the caped man's ear, then went through a door marked Staff Only. The caped man stared at us, stupefied. 'You mean to tell me you keep animals in your houses, and you don't eat them?' Some members of the class expressed their horror and outrage. The caped man wouldn't let it go. 'You treat your animals as if they are your babies?' Somebody stood and left, flinging their 'How to Play Ukelele' manual onto the floor. 'You are all mad,' the caped man said, throwing off his cape. 'Hans Werner Borgmann! The World's Greatest Ukelele Instructor!' was written on the back of his black T-shirt. 'I cannot teach you anything.' He opened his wallet and slapped our fees on the table. 'Take it!' The man with the tank top was disconsolate. 'But I'm on your side,' he said. 'Take your money. Give it to the poor. I never want to see you again,' Hans said. I shook his hand. 'That's the most decisive thing I've seen all weekend. Did you have a good night's sleep?' Hans clenched his fists, and I thought he might punch me in the solar plexus, but his fury subsided. 'I haven't slept since 1968,' he said, and picked up an out of tune ukulele. 'But through it all, I've had music.' He strummed a melody I didn't know or admire. 'One day,' he said, 'one day, the world will be ready for the ukulele.'

EVIDENCE

A short man with yellow teeth and wet hair was making his way through the Atrium in shorts and flip flops, a towel around his neck. He'd had the most rigorous of morning workouts and was blowing hard. He stopped next to me at the water cooler, where I was washing down some tablets. 'Elvis stayed in this hotel,' he said. Dr Brendan O'Flaherty joined us, impeccably kitted out in blue linen suit and crisp white shirt, no tie. 'Elvis did not stay here,' he said. 'Yes, he did. Remember when he touched down at Prestwick in 1960?' 'He never got off that plane.' 'That's what they want you to think.' 'No, that's what happened.' 'You are so naïve,' said the yellow-toothed man, scratching his over-hanging belly. Dr O'Flaherty sighed and drank his water. 'This hotel wasn't built until 1989,' he said. 'You're so gullible,' said the man. 'Elvis died in 1977,' Dr O'Flaherty said. 'If you're going to be rude and negative, I won't take you to my room and show you the evidence.' 'What evidence?' 'The memorabilia. Photos, autographs, a wooden guitar.' 'A wooden guitar?' I said. They both turned to me. 'Who are you?' they said as one. 'Nobody,' I said. Dr O'Flaherty picked up his slim briefcase and turned back to the man. 'Did your room cost extra?' he said. 'You bet,' said the man, 'and worth every penny.'

THE TWELFTH MAN

Eleven scaffolders from Carlisle, one of whom was getting married in two days, were keen to discuss my paper on 'Agency and Narrative Morality', though I hadn't raised it with them and was frankly more interested in the continual flooding of their local football ground. 'There's no way we can find a route through this impasse?' Arkwright said. 'We've been drinking for 48 hours.' 'We've eaten nothing but doughnuts for days,' Willy said with a hint of desperation. Another of the malnourished Cumbrians lifted the tablecloth. 'What are you doing down there?' he said. The head of a man who looked a lot like the bass player from The Jam popped up. 'I'm looking for a new wife,' he said. 'What's wrong with your old one,' Tinker said. 'She's not old,' the man said. 'You look like that bloke who played bass with The Jam,' Chadwick said. 'I get that a lot. My name's Badger,' The Jam bass player look-a-like said. 'Why do you need a new wife, Badger?' Montague said. Badger pulled out a sheet of paper. 'It says on this application form.' 'Let me see that,' Stefan snatched it from him. We sat quietly while he read it. He took a pencil from my breast pocket and doodled in the margin. 'It's just one of the new recommendations. It's not compulsory,' Stefan said at last. Badger was only slightly relieved. 'My wife thinks the most enjoyable aspect of being a grown up is not having to eat her crusts anymore,' Badger said. 'Yes, a wife like that would do,' Naseby said, suddenly interested in something other than his mobile phone. 'Stay away from my wife,' Badger said. He tried to stand up but was restrained by Gilligan, who also worked at the hospital radio station. 'You've given me no option now,' Naseby said.

SWINGING ON THE SECOND FLOOR

There was a buzz about the Breakfast Buffet. The queue felt like a bustling city centre during the marching season. 'She was fattening me up to take to market but I escaped,' one man said. 'I feel threatened by my former life. I'm afraid of my own ghost, he will not settle, he will not apologise,' another man said. I felt a sharp jag in my thigh. I looked down on a woman holding a geometry drafting compass. 'Did you just stab me?' She looked up, 'Don't be ridiculous,' she said. 'But now that I have your attention, have you noticed how tall everybody is these days? People didn't used to be so tall. Do you think it's all the steroids?' I caught sight of her name tag. 'Well Dara, maybe you've got shorter.' 'That's highly offensive,' she said, and stabbed me in the other thigh. Nobody in the queue said anything. A tiny blood stain appeared through my trousers. Two strapping men in black trench coats appeared on either side of her. 'Dara, are you bothering this gentleman? I'm so sorry, sir,' said the balder of the two balding men. The less bald man picked her up like a chihuahua and cradled her. She struggled a little and tried to stab him. His colleague quickly prised the compass from her. 'I want a biscuit,' she said. 'Don't worry, sir. We sterilise all her compasses every hour, on the hour.' Dara was falling asleep in his arms. 'All right then,' I said, 'I won't prosecute.' He stared down at her. 'That's very considerate,' he said without looking up. 'Do try the kedgeree this morning, it's exquisite. It reminds me of my days in the Foreign Office.' The two men stepped lightly away, carrying the sleeping Dara to her biscuits. I couldn't help thinking she was now in very safe hands.

IN THE NAME OF THE FATHER

I was on my third plate of kedgeree, watching people come and go. 'Are you giving a paper this morning?' said a young fellow, sitting down with a crowd of his peers. I was swept up in their comprehensive bonhomie. 'Why, yes!' I said. 'You know, I think I will!' He and his friends were delighted for me. 'We should come to hear it!' They banged the table in joy. Cups and bowls jumped up and down. 'Where are you speaking?' said one. 'What's it about?' said another. 'I heard your paper yesterday!' said yet another. 'Yes! It was really interesting!' I blushed and wondered whom they thought I was. 'So, where?' said one of their number, a pale boy noticeably less animated than the others. He wore his lanyard like a federal law enforcement officer. I suspected he wasn't yet a proper doctor, but a bitter postgraduate incensed by the number of corrections he had been given at his viva voce. My duplicity, so aroused by their affability, was in danger of unravelling. 'Um, Conference 9 on the Eighth Floor?' I said. 'Isn't 9 on 4?' said one. '12's on 8, surely?' 'Isn't 9 fallow this year?' 'That's Glastonbury, you tit.' 'Oh yea.' They were distracted. My spontaneous improvisation was working. I made a break for it. The whey-faced boy followed me out of the Breakfast Buffet. 'I'll report you,' he said. 'Why don't you do that,' I said. I was low on name tags, but pulled one from my pocket and waved it front of his face. 'Here, name and institution. Do your worst.' He read my details. He rubbed his eyes. 'Dad?' He blinked. I sensed my opportunity. 'See where negativity gets you, young man? Now go to your room.' He reached out to hug me. 'Now,' I said. His head dropped to his chin. 'Yes, father.' It was a close call, but I was in the clear.

THE MOBILE BOTTOM IMPLANT TRUCK

I was returning to the conference after a short stroll to clear my mind, when I came upon a queue of people in the overflow car park. 'What's going on?' I said to a couple who seemed very excited. 'It's the mobile bottom implant truck!' said the young woman. 'The what?' I said. 'Isn't it great? Nobody knows when or where it will show up,' the young man said. 'I'm sorry, but did you say, "bottom implant"?' I said. They laughed, nudging other people in the queue. 'You make it sound like you don't know what bottom implants are!' I looked at the long line of people. 'It's certainly very popular,' I said. 'Billy has finally agreed to have his done,' the young woman said, reaching for his hand. 'I had mine eight months ago. Do you like it?' she turned and bent over. 'I wouldn't have noticed if you hadn't pointed it out,' I said. They were aghast. 'Don't be sad, Tina,' the young man said. 'Do you think I should ask for an upgrade?' she said. An elderly woman pinched my arm. 'That was uncalled for,' she said to me. 'I didn't mean to upset her,' I said, rubbing my arm. 'Anyway, you're a little old for bottom implants, aren't you?' I said to her. She pinched me again. 'It's not for me, it's for Raymond,' she said. 'Who's Raymond?' I said. A head popped out from inside her coat. 'Oh my god,' I said. 'What the hell is that?' It tried to leap from her grasp and bite me, but she was strong. 'Raymond is going to be the cutest big-bottomed Terrier cross in all of Greater Manchester, aren't you darling?' she said, rubbing her nose on Raymond's. 'Does Raymond have any say in this?' I said. 'Are you some kind of simpleton?' she said. 'Raymond's just a dog.' Raymond licked her chin. She looked like she might French kiss him. I would need a second breakfast to get over this.

SKIPPING THE PLENARY

In the lobby, delegates wheeled suitcases and said rushed goodbyes as taxis drew up outside. There was a breathless, light-headed liminality in the air, like there is every Sunday. A young man stumbled into me and knocked me off my feet. A young woman helped me up as he lurched away. 'He's a bit high right now. He gave his paper this morning. It's like a drug, isn't it? Are you all right?' I nodded, though I think I might have chipped a bone in my wrist. She gripped me by my upper arms and drew me close. 'You know you can do better than this, don't you?' she said. My arms were going numb. 'I'm not a very good person,' I said. 'That's a brave declaration,' she said. 'I learned everything I know on the cricket fields of Somerset,' I said. She let go. 'I'm sorry. My mistake.' She started to follow him but stopped. 'You kid yourself that the people you meet complete you, but they just prove how alone you are,' she said. 'Come on,' I said, giving her a cinnamon twist, 'it's not that bad.' She took a bite and spat it out. 'Bollocks,' she said. 'I knew that was going to happen.' She took a slip of paper from her pocket, read it, and ripped it into several pieces. Then she took off her rings and handed me everything. 'See he gets these.' She ran off to the stairwell. The rings looked expensive. My flat was across the road from a pawnbroker. I would have to check my diary for Monday morning appointments.

THE BOOK OF CANDY

Three professors of Economics were searching their bags by Reception. 'I remember when there was no such thing as a gigabyte,' the first said, emptying his toilet bag. 'There have always been gigabytes,' the second said, lifting a heavy object out of his bag and placing it on the desk. 'Nonsense,' the first said, repacking his toilet bag and shaking out a pair of blue chinos. The second professor wiped his brow. 'Gigabytes are mentioned in the Bible,' he said. 'Gigabytes are not mentioned in the Bible,' the first professor said, un-balling his socks and feeling for something that obviously wasn't there. 'Candy 3:21,' the second said. 'Candy?' the first said. 'And Candy did feed the beast with spikes / baked in barleycorn and mustard seeds / And Gigabyte did bloat and suffer / And his belly ached and did explode / And his guts did land in the forest / And what did grow there was a great tree / And it was named the Tree of Everything,' the second said. For an instant, the first professor appeared uncertain. 'Isn't that the book of Daniel?' the third professor said. 'Didn't Daniel fight a lion?' the second said. 'Don't be silly. That was the Book of St George,' the first said. 'And it was a dragon.' 'There's no Book of St George,' the second said. 'It's Apocryphal,' the first said. 'So, who fought the lion?' the second said. 'There's a lot of fighting in the Bible, isn't there?' the third professor said. The three professors sat on their open bags and rested their chins on their hands. 'It's not a great example to set before the children, is it?' the second said. A professor of Zoology waiting to check out coughed loudly and stamped his foot with impatience, but he had misjudged the moment. Everybody was now considering the children. Checking out would never be as important as it used to be.

FIXED PENALTIES

The contents of a dozen suitcases were strewn about the car park. Windows were smashed and boots jemmied open. Drivers and passengers wandered through the mess trying to locate their belongings. 'Life seems to be so much more dangerous than it used to be,' Dinah Ullenbeck said. 'What shall we do with all the murderous children?' her friend Hazima said, picking up a crushed box of salted caramel truffles. 'The children are merely exhibiting the behaviours they have been taught,' Jăna said to Hoakins when he picked up a shattered Tiffany lamp and threw its remains at a passing Boy Scout. 'Then what shall we do with ourselves?' Hoakins said. 'We shall keep our heads down and buy shares in the government,' Jăna said. A small crowd rallied around Hoakins and consoled him. 'I didn't know we could do that,' Graeme Butler said. 'We can do anything if we know the right people,' Aivars said, taking his place beside Jăna. Christine and Meena were unimpressed. They huffed and turned their backs. 'But if we do nothing, our children shall rise up against us,' their colleague Guttierez said. A group of delegates waiting for transport to the airport joined him. 'It's either us or them. We shall have to kill our children before they kill us,' Gideon said. 'That seems to make the only sense I can understand,' Noah said. 'Let us make a pact and sign it,' Dr Carruthers said. Aivars turned to Jăna. 'Do we know the right people?' Jăna brushed some dandruff from his shoulder. 'I'm working on it,' she said.

EPILOGUE: THE WHITE HORSE

I was standing in the mist by the taxi rank when Kathrine rode up on a big black Irish Draught stallion. It must have been 17 hands high. She put out her arm. 'Jump up,' she said. We rode. The rhythm overwhelmed me. I rested my head on her shoulder.

Where are we going?
To the next town
How far is it?
A couple of days
What will we do when we get there?
We'll get another horse
We'll be tired
No, it's a white horse
Who will be there to meet us?
Just enjoy the ride
I can't
Look at the willowherb
That's weed. That's fireweed
Yes, but isn't it beautiful?

Night fell. We arrived at the next town and hitched our horse to a rail outside the bar. 'Where's the white horse?' I said. Kathrine chewed her tobacco and spat on the ground. 'I guess we're early. Let's have a drink and freshen up.' 'What if there's no white horse?' I said. 'Then we'll walk. Whatever happens, we keep going. All right?' Kathrine's spurs jingled as she pushed open the doors and strode into the bar. 'I'll get us a room. You order food. We'll set out in the morning.' They felt like good ideas. A bit of food. Keep going.

www.ingramcontent.com/pod-product-compliance
Lightning Source LLC
Chambersburg PA
CBHW011522070526
44585CB00022B/2506